CORE LIBRARY OF US STATES

Pennsylvania

BY TAMMY GAGNE
CONTENT CONSULTANT
Steve Smith
Associate Director of Research Services
Historical Society of Pennsylvania

Core Library
An Imprint of Abdo Publishing
abdobooks.com

abdobooks.com

Published by Abdo Publishing, a division of ABDO, PO Box 398166, Minneapolis, Minnesota 55439. Copyright © 2023 by Abdo Consulting Group, Inc. International copyrights reserved in all countries. No part of this book may be reproduced in any form without written permission from the publisher. Core Library™ is a trademark and logo of Abdo Publishing.

Printed in the United States of America, North Mankato, Minnesota.
052022
092022

Cover Photo: Shutterstock Images
Interior Photos: Sean Pavone/Shutterstock Images, 4–5, 43; Red Line Editorial, 7 (Pennsylvania), 7 (USA); Peter Gridley/Photodisc/Getty Images, 10–11; Emanuel Leutze/Gift of John Stewart Kennedy, 1897/Metropolitan Museum of Art, 13; GG Digital Arts/Shutterstock Images, 17 (flag); Tom Reichner/Shutterstock Images, 17 (deer); Maria Komar/Shutterstock Images, 17 (flower); Roger Hall/Science Source, 17 (firefly); Shutterstock Images, 17 (firefly background), 37; Bradley D. Saum/Shutterstock Images, 17 (tree); Jon Bilous/Shutterstock Images, 20–21; Delmas Lehman/Shutterstock Images, 24, 45; Mark Burnett/Science Source, 26–27; Gang Liu/Shutterstock Images, 31; George Sheldon/Shutterstock Images, 32; Michael Bryant/The Philadelphia Inquirer/AP Images, 34–35; Don Wright/AP Images, 40

Editor: Marie Pearson
Series Designer: Joshua Olson

Library of Congress Control Number: 2021951545

Publisher's Cataloging-in-Publication Data

Names: Gagne, Tammy, author.
Title: Pennsylvania / by Tammy Gagne
Description: Minneapolis, Minnesota : Abdo Publishing, 2023 | Series: Core library of US states | Includes online resources and index.
Identifiers: ISBN 9781532197796 (lib. bdg.) | ISBN 9781098270551 (ebook)
Subjects: LCSH: U.S. states--Juvenile literature. | Northeastern States--Juvenile literature. | Pennsylvania--History--Juvenile literature. | Physical geography--United States--Juvenile literature.
Classification: DDC 974.8--dc23

Population demographics broken down by race and ethnicity come from the 2019 census estimate. Population totals come from the 2020 census.

CONTENTS

CHAPTER ONE
The Keystone State 4

CHAPTER TWO
History of Pennsylvania 10

CHAPTER THREE
Geography and Climate 20

CHAPTER FOUR
Resources and Economy 26

CHAPTER FIVE
People and Places 34

Important Dates 42

Stop and Think 44

Glossary 46

Online Resources 47

Learn More 47

Index 48

About the Author 48

CHAPTER ONE

THE KEYSTONE STATE

A group of visitors walks toward the Liberty Bell at Independence Hall in Philadelphia, Pennsylvania. Their eyes are drawn to the giant crack down its side. The damage likely happened in the 1840s after almost 90 years of use. The bronze bell has long been an important symbol to many Americans. In the mid-1700s, it rang to call townspeople for the sharing of news. It also called lawmakers to meetings.

No one living today has ever heard the Liberty Bell ring because of its crack.

ANDREW CARNEGIE

Andrew Carnegie was born in Scotland in 1835. He was 13 when his family came to Pennsylvania. As an adult, he became one of the richest men in the world by building the US steel industry. Carnegie opened his first steel plant in Pittsburgh in 1875. His Carnegie Steel Corporation was the world's largest steel manufacturing company. Carnegie supported many causes. He built numerous free libraries. But at the same time, he made his employees work long days for low pay.

The word *liberty* means "freedom." The Liberty Bell has represented freedom for formerly enslaved Americans and equality for women in the early 1900s. Some see it fitting that the Liberty Bell resides in the Keystone State. Pennsylvania is called the Keystone State because of its role in the building of the United States.

A keystone is a wedge-shaped stone used in building arches. This stone holds all the others in place. This is how many people see Pennsylvania's role in the founding of the nation.

MAP OF PENNSYLVANIA

Take a look at the locations on this map. How does the map help you better understand Chapter One?

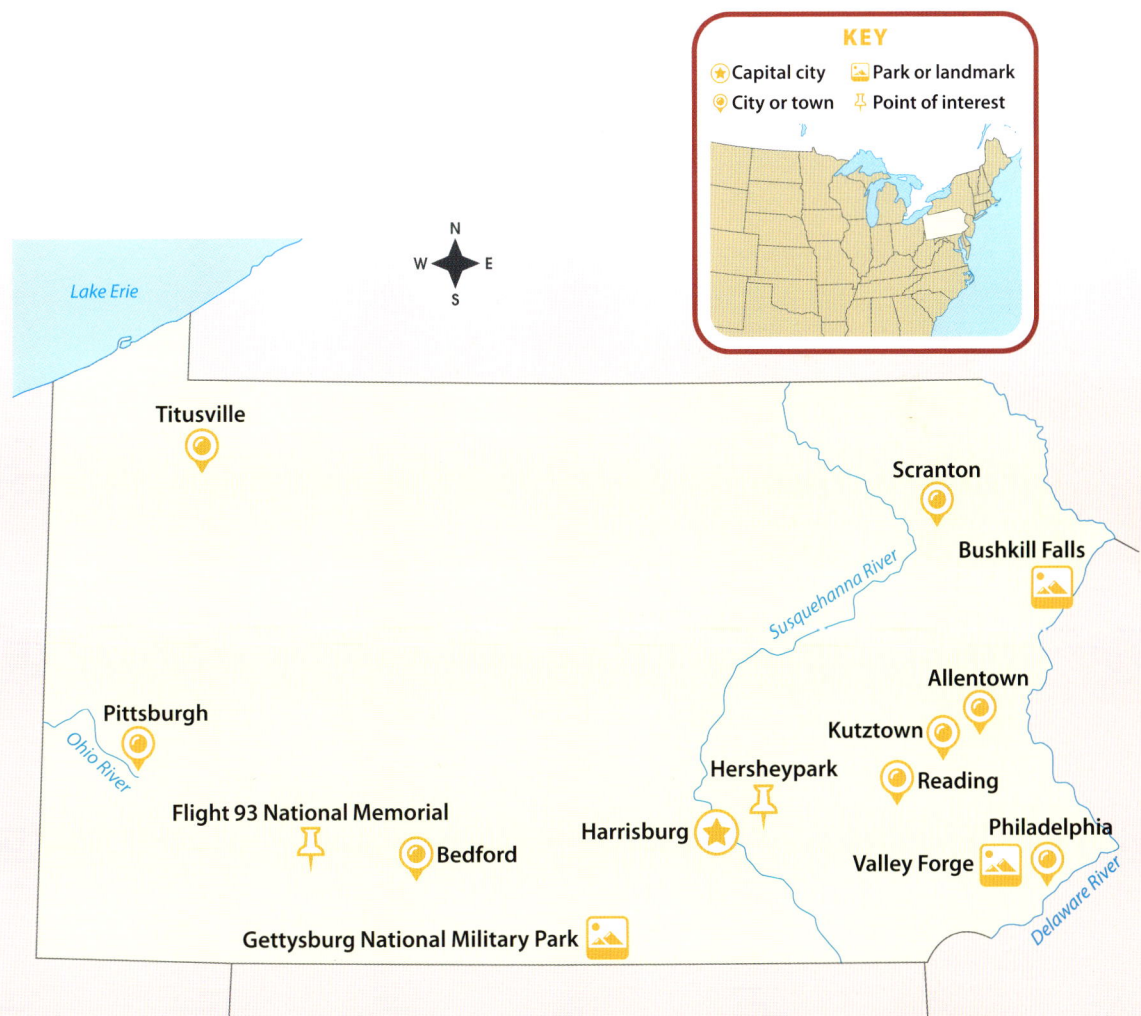

RICH IN HISTORY

Pennsylvania is part of the Mid-Atlantic region in the northeastern United States. Much of the Revolutionary War (1775–1783) was fought on this land. Pennsylvania borders six other US states. New York lies to the north and east. Also to the east is New Jersey. Delaware and Maryland lie to the south. West Virginia is located to the south and west. Ohio lies to the west. Lake Erie, one of the nation's five Great Lakes, is along the northwest border.

Philadelphia is the state's largest city. Other big cities in the state include Pittsburgh and Allentown. Pittsburgh is known as the Steel City because it once produced a lot of the useful metal. Harrisburg is the state capital. Pennsylvania is also home to many smaller towns and farming communities.

Many important documents in US history were created in Pennsylvania. The Declaration of Independence, US Constitution, and Gettysburg

Address were all written in the state. Pennsylvania was also the site of many famous battles. Today people come from all over to visit Pennsylvania's historic locations and monuments. Tourists explore historical sites such as the Gettysburg Battlefield. Many spend a day at Hersheypark, the theme park of the famous candy company. Hikers travel the many trails of the Pocono Mountains. People of all ages have plenty of choices for how to spend their time in the Keystone State.

PERSPECTIVES
PHILADELPHIA

Philadelphia is Pennsylvania's largest city. It is known as the City of Brotherly Love. The name Philadelphia was created by combining two Greek words. The word *phileo* means "love." *Adelphos* means "brother." Some supporters of gender equality have added "and sisterly affection" to the nickname. Dyana Williams is a radio broadcaster who has promoted using the updated nickname. She said, "I want young girls growing up in the city of Philadelphia knowing that they're part of it. They're part of the lifestyle, part of the mechanism of what makes Philadelphia such a cultural gem."

CHAPTER TWO

HISTORY OF PENNSYLVANIA

People have lived in Pennsylvania for at least 10,000 years. Paleo-Indians were the first-known people to occupy the region. They were nomadic hunters and gatherers who traveled to find food.

By the 1400s various American Indian peoples lived in Pennsylvania. These included the Lenape (Delaware), Susquehannock, Shawnee, and Haudenosaunee. The Lenape people lived in the area now known as Philadelphia. They hunted, fished, and farmed.

A historical image shows a meeting between William Penn and American Indians.

EUROPEAN SETTLEMENT

European settlers first arrived in Pennsylvania in the early 1600s. The first permanent European settlement in the area was the colony of New Sweden. It was established by Swedish settlers in 1638. In 1655 the Dutch seized it. Nine years later the English took control of the colony. Pennsylvania received its present name when King Charles II gave the land to William Penn in 1681. Penn hoped to make the colony a safe place for himself and other Quakers. This religious group had faced persecution in England.

Penn wanted to have good relationships with the American Indian peoples in Pennsylvania. He paid the Lenape people for the land Europeans had forcibly taken. The Quakers were pacifists. This meant they did not believe in fighting wars. When disputes happened, Penn insisted that a committee with an equal number of settlers and American Indians decide on resolutions. His efforts made relations between the groups work well for many years.

A famous painting of the Revolutionary War shows George Washington leading soldiers from Pennsylvania across the Delaware River to attack a military base in New Jersey.

The Quakers did not believe in slavery. But it was allowed under English law, and not everyone in the colony was a Quaker. Some of the colonists were slaveholders. By 1710 about 20 percent of Philadelphia's population was enslaved.

Around this time, the British controlled Pennsylvania and several other eastern colonies. But the French controlled much of the land to the north. France wanted to expand its territory in North America.

This led to the French and Indian War (1754–1763). Several battles were fought in Pennsylvania. France won many of the early battles of the war with help from American Indian nations. They included the Shawnee people of Pennsylvania. But England's greater wealth and resources helped the British win the war.

REVOLUTION

The French and Indian War cost the British a lot of money. The British government soon increased taxes on the American colonists. Many people in Pennsylvania and the other colonies became outraged. The colonists had no representation in the British government. This meant that they couldn't influence what was taxed or how much they were taxed. Tensions grew, leading to the Revolutionary War.

Many important events relating to the Revolutionary War took place in Pennsylvania. The First and Second Continental Congresses met in Philadelphia at the Pennsylvania State House. These groups of delegates from the colonies met in Pennsylvania to form a new national government. In the 1770s they created and approved the Declaration of Independence. This document announced the colonies' independence from the British. The final text was approved on July 4, 1776. The Battle of Brandywine, the Battle of Germantown, and the Continental Army's encampment at Valley Forge were all in Pennsylvania. The war was long. In 1783 the United States emerged as a free nation.

VALLEY FORGE

More than 12,000 soldiers camped at Valley Forge from December 1777 until June 1778 under the command of General George Washington. The concentration of soldiers made it easier to protect the countryside from British forces. But it was a long, hard winter. Nearly 2,000 people died when diseases spread through the camp.

Pennsylvania became the second state on December 12, 1787. It established a three-part state government that still exists today. The executive branch includes the governor, who leads the state. The General

PERSPECTIVES

A CAPITAL CITY

Philadelphia was the US capital from 1790 to 1800. But many people worried that a national capital within a state would be heavily influenced by that state's leaders on national issues. So the federal government created Washington, DC, which was not a state. In 1800 DC became the permanent US capital. Journalist Joel Rose said, "Philadelphia lost much of its political significance, though it remained an important financial center throughout the 19th century."

Assembly creates the state's laws. It includes senators and representatives. The Pennsylvania Supreme Court interprets these laws in court cases.

WARS AND STEEL

Pennsylvania was once again a key site during the Civil War (1861–1865). This war began when the United States became divided over the issue of slavery. The Northern states wanted to abolish slavery. The Southern states wanted to continue to allow it. Eleven Southern states seceded from, or left, the United States. They formed a new nation called

PENNSYLVANIA
QUICK FACTS

Examine these facts about Pennsylvania and symbols of the state. How do they help you better understand Pennsylvania?

Abbreviation: PA
Nickname: The Keystone State
Motto: Virtue, liberty, and independence
Date of statehood: December 12, 1787
Capital: Harrisburg
Population: 13,002,700
Area: 46,054 square miles (119,279 sq km)

STATE SYMBOLS

State animal
White-tailed deer

State insect
Firefly

State flower
Mountain laurel

State tree
Eastern hemlock

the Confederacy. Pennsylvania stayed in the Union and fought for the Union Army.

A major battle of the Civil War was fought near Gettysburg. The Battle of Gettysburg was a turning point in the war. The Confederate Army tried to invade the North in July 1863. But Union soldiers defeated the South in the three-day battle. President Abraham Lincoln delivered his famous Gettysburg Address on the battlefield later that year. Many Union soldiers had lost their lives in the battle. Lincoln dedicated the battlefield as a final resting place for those soldiers. The Union won the war in 1865. The United States officially abolished slavery that year.

The United States relied heavily on the US steel industry during World War II (1939–1945). Steel was needed for military supplies. It was used to make airplanes, warships, guns, and ammunition.

Pennsylvania accounted for more than 30 percent of the steel produced in the United States during the war. The city of Pittsburgh was already famous for its steel. But a world war demanded even more than the city alone could provide. Bethlehem Steel in the town of Bethlehem also provided a large amount of the material needed for the war effort. Today steel is a much smaller industry in the state. But companies continue to produce it.

FURTHER EVIDENCE

Chapter Two discusses the Battle of Gettysburg. What was one of the main points? What evidence is included to support this point? Read the article at the website below. Does the information on the website support this point? Does it present new evidence?

THE BATTLE OF GETTYSBURG
abdocorelibrary.com/pennsylvania

CHAPTER THREE

GEOGRAPHY AND CLIMATE

Hills and valleys make up much of Pennsylvania's geography. The state is divided by the Appalachian Mountains. In Pennsylvania, this mountain range includes the Allegheny and Pocono Mountains. The only lowlands are in the southeast corner of the state. More than half of Pennsylvania is forested.

The state has more than 86,000 miles (138,000 km) of rivers, streams, and creeks. With the exception of Alaska, this is more

The Pocono Mountains are full of beautiful features, including waterfalls.

than any other US state. Major rivers include the Ohio, Delaware, and Susquehanna. The Delaware River forms the border between Pennsylvania and New Jersey. Lake Erie is the largest lake Pennsylvania touches.

Pennsylvania borders 63 miles (101 km) of the lake's shoreline.

VALLEY AND RIDGE PROVINCE

The Valley and Ridge Province is located in eastern Pennsylvania. This area is made up of many long, narrow valleys and ridges between the Appalachian Mountains. The valleys formed from the erosion of soft rock over hundreds of millions of years. The remaining ridges are areas of harder stone that better withstood the wind and water.

CLIMATE AND WEATHER

Pennsylvania has a temperate climate. The weather is hot in the summer and cold in the winter. Summer days are usually 75 to 95 degrees Fahrenheit (24–35°C). Winter days range from 33 to 45 degrees Fahrenheit (0.6–7°C). The western part of the state is colder than the east. It also gets more rain and snow each year. The different seasons offer Pennsylvanians a wide range of outdoor activities.

Snowstorms are common in winter. Spring rains often lead to flooding. Fog can be thick in the valleys in any season. In recent years Pennsylvania has experienced more tornadoes. Experts say this is due to climate change. Most tornadoes occur in the month of July.

WILDLIFE

A wide variety of flowers, plants, and trees grow in Pennsylvania. The state flower is the mountain laurel.

PERSPECTIVES
A FORBIDDEN HIKE

Glen Onoko Falls Trail has attracted visitors since the 1800s. But many people have fallen while climbing on the slippery rocks to get a better look at the trail's waterfall. Several of them died. The Pennsylvania Game Commission decided to close the trail in 2019 for safety reasons. Nature lovers such as Brandon Huffman disagreed with the decision. He said, "Nature can be dangerous. You just have to have your wits about you and have some common sense."

Some elk live in Elk County in Pennsylvania.

These shrubs grow up to 10 feet (3 m) tall. They develop pink-and-white blooms each year from late May until mid-June. Mountain laurels grow wild throughout the state. Many people also grow this shrub in their gardens. Pennsylvania's state tree is the Eastern hemlock. This evergreen with a massive trunk was widely used throughout Pennsylvania's history. Early American colonists built cabins with its wood. People used its bark for tanning leather.

Pennsylvania is home to the largest elk herd in the Northeast. This majestic species had disappeared from the state by 1867 due to hunting and habitat loss. The Pennsylvania Game Commission began reintroducing the species to the area in 1913. Elk sightings are now common in the spring, summer, and fall. The state is also known for its large deer population. The white-tailed deer is the state animal of Pennsylvania. Hunting both elk and deer is a popular fall and early winter activity. On summer nights, the Pennsylvania firefly glows in fields and woodlands.

EXPLORE ONLINE

Chapter Three discusses Pennsylvania's elk population. The website below focuses on the same topic. As you know, every source is different. How is the information at the website different from the information in this chapter? What information is the same? What information did you learn from the website?

ELK VIEWING TIPS
abdocorelibrary.com/pennsylvania

CHAPTER FOUR

RESOURCES AND ECONOMY

Pennsylvania has an abundance of natural resources. Large amounts of coal, oil, natural gas, and metals are found in the state. Each of these items plays a big role in Pennsylvania's economy. Pennsylvania is the only state to mine anthracite coal. This hard coal burns hotter than any other type of coal. The state is one of the top producers of natural gas in the nation. Only Texas produces more. This energy source heats about half the homes in Pennsylvania.

A dam on the Susquehanna River generates hydropower.

> ## STRIKING OIL
> Pennsylvania was the center of oil production in the mid-1800s. Edwin L. Drake drilled the first successful well in the nation in 1859. The rest of the world followed as oil became one of the most popular energy sources around the globe. Visitors to Pennsylvania can learn about Drake and his efforts at the Drake Well Museum and Park in Titusville.

The state also sends natural gas to other parts of the country.

Pennsylvania produces renewable energy too. The state uses its rivers for hydropower. Water flows into pipes at hydropower plants. It then pushes against blades to spin a generator, which produces electricity. Hydropower is Pennsylvania's biggest source of renewable energy.

AGRICULTURE

Agriculture is another large part of the state's economy. More than 2,300 food processing businesses operate in Pennsylvania. Most farms are in rural areas, such as York, Lancaster, and Berks Counties. But farms are found in every Pennsylvania county.

Pennsylvania has rich soil that is perfect for growing crops such as corn, oats, and soybeans. The state is also a top grower of apples and mushrooms. Other Pennsylvania farms focus on raising animals. Many of these businesses produce beef, eggs, and milk.

INDUSTRY

Pennsylvania serves as the headquarters of several large companies. One is the

PERSPECTIVES

AMISH COUNTRY

Amish country in Lancaster County essentially has its own economy. The Amish are a group of Christians who came to Pennsylvania from Europe in the early 1700s. Amish people reject most forms of modern technology. They live mostly separate lives from other Pennsylvanians. But they bring money into their community from the rest of the world. Many Amish people work on farms. Others specialize in craftsmanship. Amish dolls, quilts, and furniture are all popular. The area has also become a tourist site. As economics author Martin Lutz pointed out, "Online shops now ship Amish furniture abroad, and tourist agencies brand Amish country as a destination for international travelers."

Hershey chocolate company. In 1905 Milton Hershey built a chocolate plant in a town called Derry Church. His milk chocolate bar quickly became a huge success. The Hershey Company now makes more than $8 billion in yearly sales worldwide. And the town of Derry Church is now known as Hershey.

Comcast is a giant in cable television, entertainment, and communications. In 1969 the company moved to Philadelphia. By 2018 Comcast employed more than 12,000 people in the Greater Philadelphia region. Kraft Heinz is another large business in Pennsylvania. Its headquarters are split between Pittsburgh and Chicago, Illinois. Kraft Heinz produces food products that are sold all over the world.

TOURISM

Pennsylvania's tourism industry is a big moneymaker. Each year, more than 200 million people from around the United States travel to Pennsylvania.

Philadelphia is home to many companies. It is also a popular place for tourism.

Hersheypark is a popular family theme park.

Another 2.3 million come from other countries. In all, these tourists spend more than $43 billion in Pennsylvania each year.

Some tourists go to Pennsylvania to see historic sites such as the Gettysburg National Military Park or the Liberty Bell. Others want to visit Hersheypark. Still others explore the state's mountain ranges and nature preserves. Tourism helps keep more than half a million people employed in the state.

STRAIGHT TO THE
SOURCE

Agricultural economics professor Timothy W. Kelsey and student Emily O'Coonahern wrote an article about Pennsylvania's farming industry. In it they said:

> *Many Pennsylvania farms sell directly to customers through roadside stands and farmers' markets. . . .*
>
> *Roadside stands are always fun places to visit because you can talk directly with the farmers who grew the food and buy locally grown produce. Some farmers sell specialty products they've developed with their crops, such as jams, salsas, pies, or even chocolate-covered apples. Some roadside farm stands have fun activities to do, such as corn mazes, petting zoos, hayrides, or pick-your-own pumpkin patches.*
>
> Source: Timothy W. Kelsey and Emily O'Coonahern. "The Joy of Farm Watching." *Penn State Extension*, 12 Sept. 2017, extension.psu.edu. Accessed 22 July 2021.

WHAT'S THE BIG IDEA?

Take a close look at the authors' words. What is their main idea? What evidence is used to support this point? Write a few sentences showing how the authors use two or three pieces of evidence to support their main point.

CHAPTER
FIVE

PEOPLE AND PLACES

More than 13 million people live in Pennsylvania. About 75 percent of them are white people who are not Hispanic or Latino. About 12 percent of the population is Black. Nearly 8 percent are Hispanic or Latino, and almost 4 percent are Asian. American Indians also live in the state. Immigrants make up about 7 percent of the state's population. Another 9 percent have at least one parent who came to the United States from another country. The most

The ODUNDE Festival is held in one of Philadelphia's oldest historically Black neighborhoods.

PERSPECTIVES
FIGHTING DISCRIMINATION

More than 200,000 people took part in the March on Washington in 1963 to protest racial discrimination. One of its organizers was Bayard Rustin, who was born in West Chester. Rustin spent much of his life fighting discrimination through nonviolent protests. But because he was gay, many history books did not mention him. Although Rustin died in 1987, President Barack Obama honored him with the Presidential Medal of Freedom in 2013. Obama spoke about the unfairness with which Rustin was treated. He said, "No medal can change that, but today we honor Bayard Rustin's memory by taking our place in his march toward true equality, no matter who we are or who we love."

common countries of origin are India, the Dominican Republic, China, and Mexico.

The state hosts several festivals that highlight its diverse cultures. The ODUNDE Festival in Philadelphia is one of the largest and longest-running African American street festivals in the country. It draws as many as 500,000 people each June. It includes live music, vendors, and African art.

People can enjoy a variety of foods and drinks at the Kutztown Folk Festival.

The Kutztown Folk Festival is the oldest folk festival in the nation. Every summer, it celebrates Pennsylvania Dutch heritage. The Pennsylvania Dutch are known for being exceptional craftspeople. Quilts sold at this annual festival often attract buyers from all over the world.

One of the state's most scenic celebrations is Bedford's Fall Foliage Festival. This October celebration invites visitors to the mountains of central Pennsylvania. The vibrant colors of the fall leaves are the perfect backdrop for enjoying crafts, live music, and tasty fall treats.

Many famous people come from the state. One of the most famous people from Pennsylvania went on to live in the White House. President Joe Biden was born in Scranton. He and his family lived there for the first several years of his life. Taylor Swift is from Reading. She moved to Nashville, Tennessee, as a teenager to pursue a musical career. Her song "Seven" features her home state. Actor Will Smith grew up in West Philadelphia.

PLACES TO VISIT

Pennsylvania has many important historical sites. Independence Hall and the Benjamin Franklin National Memorial are two of the most popular. Some people visit the statue of Fred Rogers, who hosted the TV show

Mister Rogers' Neighborhood, in Pittsburgh. He was born in the nearby city of Latrobe.

Outdoorsy people enjoy trips to the Pocono Mountains. The area offers many fun activities, from whitewater rafting to zip-lining. Hikers can make an afternoon of exploring Bushkill Falls. The site spans 300 acres (120 ha) and includes eight waterfalls.

Pennsylvanians are passionate about sports. The state has eight major-league teams. Basketball fans cheer for the Philadelphia 76ers. Baseball fans gather for Philadelphia

FLIGHT 93

A somber memorial in the state is the Flight 93 National Memorial in Stoystown. On September 11, 2001, terrorists took control of the plane. They planned to crash the plane into the White House. But the crew and passengers fought the terrorists. The plane crashed in an empty Pennsylvania field. Everyone on board was killed. Visitors at the memorial pay their respects to the brave people who kept the plane from reaching the White House that morning.

The Pittsburgh Steelers play at Heinz Field.

Phillies or Pittsburgh Pirates games. Soccer enthusiasts enjoy a Philadelphia Union game. Football fans watch the Philadelphia Eagles or the Pittsburgh Steelers. Hockey lovers flock to Philadelphia Flyers or Pittsburgh Penguins games.

Pennsylvania's wide range of sites and activities make the state an ideal vacation destination. From learning more about US history to exploring nature, there is always something worthwhile to do in the Keystone State.

STRAIGHT TO THE SOURCE

Sierra Binduga was a college freshman when she visited the Flight 93 National Memorial in 2019. After the experience, she wrote:

The part that truly stuck out to me was the wall of pictures in the Visitor Center. I saw this as a way of showing how the victims lived. They are all linked with how they died, but if you dig deeper, you will find that Lauren Grandcolas was just three months pregnant, Hilda Marcin escaped Nazi Germany when she was 6 years old, and Todd Beamer had two boys and a baby on the way. . . . We remember these names and the 36 others because this story is about them. This isn't the story of terrorists who broke America. It's the story of terrorists who couldn't estimate the courage in the victims' hearts.

Source: "Altoona Student Shares Thoughts on Flight 93 Visit." *Penn State*, 9 Oct. 2019, news.psu.edu. Accessed 22 July 2021.

BACK IT UP

The author of this passage is using evidence to support a point. Write a paragraph describing the point the author is making. Then write down two or three pieces of evidence the author uses to make the point.

IMPORTANT DATES

10,000 years ago
Paleo-Indians lived in the area now known as Pennsylvania.

1600s
Europeans arrive in Pennsylvania.

1638
New Sweden, the first permanent European settlement in the area, is established in Pennsylvania.

1681
King Charles II gives land in Pennsylvania to William Penn.

1775–1783
The Revolutionary War takes place. Some battles happen in Pennsylvania. The Declaration of Independence is written and approved by the Continental Congress in the colony.

1787
Pennsylvania becomes the second state on December 12.

1861–1865
The Civil War takes place. The Battle of Gettysburg is fought in the state in 1863.

1905
Milton Hershey opens a chocolate plant.

2001
Flight 93 crashes in Pennsylvania on September 11.

STOP AND
THINK

Tell the Tale

Chapter One discusses a trip to Independence Hall to see the Liberty Bell. Imagine that you are among the tour group. Write 200 words about your experience. Describe what you see and hear, as well as how you feel standing at such an important historical site.

Surprise Me

Chapter Two discusses the history of Pennsylvania. After reading this book, what two or three facts about Pennsylvania history did you find most surprising? Write a few sentences about each fact. Why did you find each fact surprising?

Dig Deeper

After reading this book, what questions do you still have about Pennsylvania's wildlife? With an adult's help, find a few reliable sources that can help you answer your questions. Write a paragraph about what you learned.

Take a Stand

Quakers do not believe in using violence, including war. What do you think? Are there times when violence is necessary? Or do you think it is never right to use violence? Why?

GLOSSARY

abolish
to officially end something

delegate
a person representing others

discrimination
when people treat others differently based on certain factors such as appearance

economy
a place's system of goods, services, money, and jobs

erosion
the wearing away of something by the movement of wind, water, or other natural forces

nomadic
having no set home but traveling from place to place, often with the seasons to find food

persecution
ill treatment, especially due to one's religious beliefs

somber
serious and grave

temperate
a climate that does not have extremely hot or cold temperatures

ONLINE RESOURCES

To learn more about Pennsylvania, visit our free resource websites below.

Visit **abdocorelibrary.com** or scan this QR code for free Common Core resources for teachers and students, including vetted activities, multimedia, and booklinks, for deeper subject comprehension.

Visit **abdobooklinks.com** or scan this QR code for free additional online weblinks for further learning. These links are routinely monitored and updated to provide the most current information available.

LEARN MORE

Micklos, John, Jr. *Pennsylvania*. Cavendish Square, 2020.

Wesley, Caroline. *Pittsburgh Pirates*. Abdo, 2019.

INDEX

agriculture, 8, 11, 28–29, 33
American Indians, 11–12, 14, 35
Amish people, 29
animals and plants, 17, 23–25

Bedford, 7, 38
Bushkill Falls, 7, 39

Carnegie, Andrew, 6
climate, 22–23

energy, 27–28
Europeans, 12–15, 29

famous people, 38
festivals, 36–38
Flight 93 National Memorial, 7, 39, 41

Gettysburg, 7, 8–9, 18, 19, 32

Harrisburg, 7, 8, 17
Hersheypark, 7, 9, 32

immigrants, 35

Liberty Bell, 5–6, 32

mountains, 9, 21, 22, 32, 38–39

parks, 7, 9, 23, 28, 32
Philadelphia, 5, 7, 8, 9, 11, 13–14, 16, 30, 36, 38–40
Pittsburgh, 6, 7, 8, 19, 30, 39–40

rivers, 7, 21–22, 28
Rustin, Bayard, 36

sports, 39–40
steel, 6, 8, 18–19

tourism, 9, 29, 30–32

Valley Forge, 7, 15

wars, 8, 12, 14–19

About the Author

Tammy Gagne has written hundreds of books for both adults and children. Some of her recent books have been about media literacy and mental health. She lives in northern New England with her husband, her son, and several pets.